CONTEMPORARY INDIAN WOMEN NOVELISTS IN ENGLISH

-A CRITICAL ANALYSIS

DR S JAYANTHI

Contents

Preface *v*

Acknowledgements *vii*

1. Draupadi's Perspective In Chitra Banerjee Divakaruni's The Palace Of Illusions 1
2. Historical And Cultural Labyrinth Of The Subcontinent In Gita Hariharan's The Thousand Faces Of Night 18
3. Culture Conflicts In Rajam Krishnan's Lamps In The Whirlpool 33
4. Feminist Perspective In Arundhati Roy's The God Of Small Things 50

Preface

In recent years the Indian English Literature has made conspicuous progress in all its forms, mainly in fiction. Many Indian English Writers have won awards, appreciation and wide readership in India and abroad in the recent past. In the course of seeking basic information, I have consulted a number of books, book reviews, articles, etc., web-based sources are also profusely consulted. The present book is a modest attempt to present a critical analysis of some selected and celebrated novels of contemporary Indian women novelists in English. This book has covered all the novels selected in research perspective. The detailed textual study of these novels might help the research scholars and university students.

Acknowledgements

To God, for your loving guidance and for the many blessings you have bestowed upon me. I would like to thank MS.V.Srija, MA(Eng.).,MA(JMC).,MBA(HR).,PGDCE., MPhil., (PhD)., for reviewing the draft and providing her valuable inputs that helping me coming out with this book. I am equally grateful to my husband S.Arunkumar,BA.,BL., for his inspiration and guidance. I am deeply beholder to my parents and other family members for their moral support and blessings. I am thankful to Notion Press, book publisher for bringing out this book.

CHAPTER ONE

Draupadi's Perspective in Chitra Banerjee Divakaruni's The Palace of Illusions

In Indian English Literature Mythology of India is one of the greatest analytic of Indian culture. Chitra Banerjee Divakaruni has triumphantly examined the affluent culture legacy of India. Always since India has been a field of mythology which consist of the Mahabharata and Ramayana which stayed survivable the test of time for many years. Ramayana and Mahabharata are mythological novels, Divakaruni reveals mythological of women's characters. She was concerned about the fables and just a few of the books. In British literature some books concentrate on mystery plays and the marvel pursuing their steps, Indian Literature more has germinated important happens which greatness full the skills of imagination and unearthly components. This study of myth and stories are specifically handled with an explanation from the novelChitra Banerjee Divakaruni's *The Palace of Illusions.*

Chitra Banerjee Divakaruni was born in Kolkatta (then Calculla) on 29 July 1956. Her Father Rajendra Kumar Banerjee, and her mother Jatini Banerjee, she spent the first nineteen years of her life in India. Banerjee's mother was a school teacher and her father was an accountant by profession. Divakaruni was studied school at Loreto house. Then she studied Bachelor of degree in English at Presidency College, University of Calcutta in 1976. She got Master degree in United States from university in Dayton. In 1984 she received her Ph.D in English from the California University at Berkeley.

Divakaruni's major novels are '*Queen of Dream*', '*Sister of my Heart*', '*The Mistress of Spice*' *and* '*Palace of Illusion*'. Her greatest part of the novel is written for adults. 'The Brotherhood of the Conch', this novel has also written for young adult fantasy and also these novels. 'The conch Bearer' was superseded for the bluebonnet Award of 2003. The third and final ensue 'Shadow land' was published in 2009. Divakaruni's latest novel for adults 'The palace of illusion' is the re-telling of the epic. 'The Palace Illusion' consists mythological event in the female character Mahabharata is an epic novel, in which Divakaruni significance female character 'Draupadi'.

The Mahabharata is the prolonged known epic verse. Their lengthy versions comprise of over 100,000 or 200,000 unique poem lines and long prose paragraphs. The epic comprises about 110,000 couplets in eighteen divisions. The Bhagavad Gita, a conversation between Arjuna and Krishna is a part of the Mahabharata. About 1.8 million words in aggregate, Mahabharata in almost ten times the protracted of the Odyssey and Iliad unify or about four times the longest of the Ramayana.

Chitra Banerjee Divakaruni's *'The Palace of Illusion'* was a re-making and reformats of the universal famous epic *Mahabharata* and it is Divakaruni's latest novel for adults. 'The Palace of Illusion' is a re-telling of the Indian epic, this novel expressed the point of view from a marvels woman Panchali . Pertinently to today's battle ragged world. Generally epic got myths, imagination and divine wonders. 'The Palace of Illusion' derives us back to time that is wholly magical, half history and half myth. In the novel, the protagonist is Panchali the wife of the legendary Pandavas brother in the epic of Mahabharata. The novel signifies the princess Panchali's life. The novel provides us with a strange explanation of these ancient traditional tales. In beginning Panchali birth from fire. She is birth with fire mythological woman by divinely. She follows her bravery, spirit and balancing act as a woman with five husbands who have been deceived out of their father's kingdom. Panchali is a princess of Panchalam country and the daughter of Panchalam's king Durupadan. She purified into their investigation to correct their birth right non-extend at their page through year of universalize and an atrocious civil war implication all the important kings of India. Meantime we never lose view of her important duel. Struggle with her mother-in-law, her intriguing Krishna, Panchali's stealthy gravitational to the mysterious man who is her husband's most perilous enemy. Panchali is the boldest and most fiery woman, she meets terrible events in her life. Her divine name is Traupadi, she is a fiery female threatened fours a universal of Kemp, divinity and ever managing hand of fate. Myth takes their specific shapes from the cultural environment in which they grow. Myth is in general universal. Similar motifs are found in different mythologies and certain pictures that act again in the myths of people broadly divided in time and place have a general meaning or more accurately tend to elicit comparable psychological responses and serve cultural functions. Such motifs and images are called archetypes. The proud and angry heroine Draupadi has remained an enigmatic woman of substance. The characters in the epics behave with the vivacity of real and genuine life. Bheeshma, the exhaustive warrior: the reverent Drona the incapacious but stalwartKarna, Duryodhana whose restive arrogance is solvency by wide courage in deuce and the superior-souled Pandavas with deity-like vigorous as well as the power of misery; Draupadi, the most adversity of queens; Kunti the esteemed mother of heroes. Gandhari, the loyal wife sad mother of the baddish sons of Dhritarashtra are some of the abiding figures in the group, but never confound reduplicate. Then there is a noble Krishna himself most powerful of men, whose devotional and divinity through a cloud of highly human significance. His high targeting penetrated the entire epic. One can read even a rendering and feel the defeat power of the unequal wideness and predominance of the poem.

Draupadi was volcanic and decrease her opponents to the ashes. This emitting princess bent on revenge could be sympathetic and generous too. Draupadi had developed the strength to bear the trials of life. She had decided firmly not to damage the good people, and not to bend before the vicious. Draupadi was a woman, but she became as popular as the heroic Pandavas because of such a decision.

Her personality was one of lightning and thundering. This unforgettable heroine is in no way less than Beema or Arjuna in boldness, strength and sprite, velour and virtue. Her tale is a saga of misery and humiliation but she took everything in her stride and overcome each one of the perpetrators of her disgrace and agony. In the novel, Chitra Banerjee Divakaruni provides the Mahabharata from Draupadi's phases. The tale begins with her birth. Dhaima is the personal waitress of Draudpathi and She mentions about how Draupadi was born. Drupada, King of Panchaal needed to get vengeance on Drona and so he enables and composes a Yaga. Afterwards a month Dhristadyumna is the originally to arise from the fire, and he is pursued by Draupadi. Drupad is convivial for the visit of Dhristadyumna and he is neither sad nor happy for Draupadi. He gave importance to Dhristadyumna. But Dhristadyumna performs as a best brother to Draupadi. He preaches her in all situations. She is sensing that Dhristadyumna is over-conserved of her. She feels, "His weakness was that he believed completely in his destiny and has resigned himself to fulfilling it" (Divakaruni 11). As Draupadi swarthy, the other wives of Drupada did not care for her. They do not permit their children to talk to her.

Draupadi fell sorrowed. Draupadi had the best relationship with Krishna. In case, the cause may be because they are both dark skinned. Though Krishna is darker than her, he does not refer his color as a defect. He interests the heart of women with his attraction. Though others do not take care of Draupadi, she lapsed her time with her brother Dhristadyumana. Draupadi focuses to learn archery after watching her brother, but Dhaima does not want her to train such things.

Dhristadyumana tells her that women should only listen and concern to their husbands. But Draupadi objects and posits that she desires to make a life for herself. Dhristadyumna is the only companion of Draupadi. Dhristadyumana persistently remonstrates Draupadi by saying, "The problem with you is, you are too pretty for your own good. It will get you into trouble with men sooner or later, if you are not careful," (25)

One day through her waitress, Draupadi listen that there is a sage, who prognosticated the future. She begs with Dhaima to get her to the sage. It is Vyasa whom she meets there. Vyasa typifies that she would marry five husbands and become the queen of queens. He also tells that she would be the reason for battle. Many of the women would become widows because of her. He also tells that she would deplore a lot. He prophesies,

You will be remembered for causing the greatest battle of your time. You will bring about the deaths of evil kings and your children's and your brother's. A million women would become widows because of you,Yes, indeed, you will lcavc a mark on hi3tory. You will bc lovcd, though you will not always recognize who loves you. Despite your five husband, you will die alone, abandoned at the end – and yet not so. - (Divakaruni 39)

Draupadi feels sorrow after hearing his words. Dhaima consoles her that, it is impossible for the women to get married to five husbands. So his words are not true.

The next day morning when Draupadi wakes up, she looks like a witch standing in front of her. The witch conforms and promises Draupadi that she would learn her something about life. Draupadi obeyed the words of the witch. She teaches her how to talk with the person who is higher than her and also to comprehend through experience all miseries that she becomes to face. Dhaima is dander and she tells Draupadi that witch is agonizing her and the Princess could not comprehend all the miseries like sleeping down, walking without shoes, etc. But Draupadi wants to be private.

On the next day, the palace is busy and when Draupadi asks about the vexation, Dhaima tells her that it is her brother who comes back after he had gone to the forest in his childhood. And she tells about the tale of Sikhandi that she is the rebirth of Ambha and she vowed to kill Bheema. So that she went to a forest and commit Yaga to transition herself into a male. Draupadi is horrified to hear this. Sikhandi desires to see Draupadi once he comes back to the palace. She meets Sikhandi and they talk about life in common. According to Sikhandi, "The power of man is like a bull's church, while the power of a woman moves aslant, like a serpent seeking its prey" (52)

And the next day when Draupadi is alone, Dhristayumna tells her that her father had provision swayamvara and she compels to select a partner for her. Draupadi is shocked and she tells that it is father who should select a partner for his daughter. Dhristadyumna tells her that Drupad wished to make it grand an extensive so that he invited every king in Bharat and Draupadi's brother pictures every king. Draupadi is in expectation to see the picture of Arjun who is the greatest warrior and no one in the world could overcome him. When Dhristadyumna exhibit all the pictures to Draupadi, she could see the little picture of Karna sitting along with the picture of Duryodhana. She feels emotionally imagine towards him. She says,

His eyes are filled with an ancient sadness. They pulled me into them my impatience evaporated. I no longer cared to see Arjune's portrait. Instead I wanted to know how those eyes would look if the man smiled. Absurdly, I wanted to be reason for him smile. (Divakaruni 69)

She likes the picture of Karna and when she asked the drawing artist to draw the picture of Karna, Krishna does not prefer Draupadi to see that picture. Dhristadyumna tells her that it is Karna, who is the only adventuresome person in the world evenly to Arjuna. When Krishna, who is the only martial person in the universal equal to Arjuna. When Krishna asks the drawing artists to draw the picture of Pandavas, the artist replies that they are dead and there was no use of drawing their picture. Draupadi is horrified to hear that they are decedents and she is distempered whom she would get married.

Draupadi's brother Dhristadyumna, though he is not wishing to tell her the tale of Karna that one day there is a contest between Kauravas and Pandavas. Arjuna is the one who could not be overcome by others. Duryodhana invited Arjuna to a single fight, and at that time Karna is introduced. The people of Pandava's side there oppose him because Karna is the son of the chariot driver. On hearing this Duryodhana gave away the land of Anga to Karna making him the king of Anga. When Draupadi queried him if Karna got victory in swayamvara whom she would marry, Dhristadyumna get vexation, telling him that she should not select him and she should only marry Arjuna, Draupadi was impressed with Karna and she commenced thinking about him.

On the day of Swayamvara, Draupadi costumed and dressed neatly and Dhristadyumna took her to the court. He introduces some of the especial kings to Draupadi. When the contest starts, everyone efforts their best to shoot the eyes of the fish, but they could not shoot targeted point. When Karna comes onward to steer arrow, Dhristadyumna is decisive that he would shoot it accurately so, he inhibits him from the contest. When Karna is vexatious, Krishna intimates Draupadi to take adduct over the situation. Draupadi asks Karna that if she becomes his wife she should know his birth.

As Karna could not reply he feels that he is offended. Draupadi feels worried to insult Karna, she feels that Karna would be vexation with her. Later she feels worried about her actions "My disobedient heart kept going back to Karna, to that most unfortunate moment in his life" (78). Her action shocks everyone present, but Draupadi is the most affected. On meeting Karna for the first time, she feels,

I longed to look Karna's face, to see if those eyes are indeed as sad as the artist had portrayed. But even I knew hoe improper that would be. I focused instead on his hands, the wrists disdainfully bare of Ornaments, powerful the battered knuckles. If my brother had known how badly I wanted touch them, he would have been furious.(Divakaruni 93)

After publicly humiliating him, she feels guilty and compassion for the action, "My head was still awhirl with what I had done to karna. There was pain in my chest, as though someone had taken my heart in his hands and was writing it."(100) There comes a Brahmin who wants to shoot and he succeeds by shooting the eyes of the fish. Draupadi was astonished that how the Brahmin could have so much skill within him.

The Brahmin takes Draupadi by the walk without slippers and by wearing normal cotton sarees. Draupadi sees it difficult to go and she recognizes that if she had married Karna, he would not resign her to suffer like this. When the Brahmin sees that Draupadi physical of the Brahmin, she recognizes that it is nobody other than Arjun. And he takes her to the home to introduce her to his mother. Kunti, at first preference to help her with cooking, Draupadi recognizes that and she makes a perfect good dish.

Arjuna introduces Draupadi to his other brothers. When they go home and call out to Kunti to exhibit what they bought, Kundi without looking tells them to share whatever they have bought. They are horrified to hear this. When Kundi comes to know this, she wants the Draupadi should get married to all five of her sons Pandavas. Arjuna is horrified, but he could not express anything. Draupadi feels sorrowful that Arjuna did not express anything. Then all go to Drupada to inform about their wedding to Draupadi. When Drupada listens that Draupadi getting married to five brothers, he is horrified and he objected and harshly opposed it. Kundi tells him that if he did not accept Draupadi to get married to Pandavas, She could stay there in their place. Drupada hearing this, allowed for the wedding. Draupadi feels sorrowful that Arjuna is vexation with her because of this wedding.

After the wedding gets over, Vyasa tells them that Draupadi would stay with each husband for a year. Then years later, she gives birth to five sons for each of the Pandavas. When Bheesma queries Duryodhana to separate the kingdom he denied it. As there is no more offer and choice for Duryodhan, he gave them some barren land with full of snakes. When the Pandavas went to the land and cleaned and regulate it. Arjuna nabbed Maya who stayed there. When Maya requires Arjuna to release him, Arjuna orders Maya to build a palace for them based on their taste. Maya builds a beautiful palace for them, warning them not to allow anyone comes to the palace, and it will end in disturb.

One day when Narada comes to their palace, he informed Pandavas that their grand fathers are in hell and if they do the Rajasuyayaga they would go to heaven. As it is endangered and arduous to drive and manage the yaga, they want to perform this for their grandmother. So, they invite all the kings in Bharat, Dhitarashtra sent a letter to Pandavas that he could not come but his son Duryodhana with all his brothers would attend. On the last day of the yaga, Pandavas are asked to select the guest of honor.

They could not select thought they thought day night. So they query Bheesma to select the guest of honor as he is the eldest of all. When Bheesma selects Krishna as the legates of honor, Sisupal, king of chedis gets resentment and starts scolding Krishna. Krishna in anger killed Sisupal.

Duryodhana convict to stay in that palace as a guest. One day when he is walking around the palace, he could see a pond, but it is not pristine, it is an illusion. So he steps into that and fell down, Draupadi with her waitress watched and began laughing at him. At once Draupadi recognizes that Karna is along with Duryodhana, and she began laughing at him. When kundi comes to know this, she got vexation with Draupadi and orders her to ask forgive to Duryodhana. But Draupadi decides to ask forgive if it becomes a large problem. Duryodhana does not tell this to anyone and when the day comes he decides to come back to his palace.

After some months Duryodhana invites Drupad and the Pandavas to their place. Pandavas are dither because the kings should only be invited not the queens. Kunti does not desire Draupadi to go to Hastinapur. Kunti is vexation at Draupadi because she does not obey her words. When they reach Hastinapur they are invited in a good manner and they are given courtesy. As rapidly as Draupadi goes there her heart starts finding for Karna. But she could not find him. That night Pandavas are invited by the Kauravas for a dinner party. Draupadi is sure that Karna would join the party. So she instructed to make a good dress for her.

As soon as the dress comes, her heart warns that she has got married to Pandavas and it is not her work to attract Karna. So she wears a normal dress and goes to the party. There she meets Kunti, when they both are talking Karna comes near them and wishes Kunti and Draupadi, but Draupadi does not reply to him as Kunti is near. She feels sad that Karna would think she is ill-mannered. The next day, Yudhistir is called by Duryodhana for the dice game. Draupadi warns Yudhistir not to drink too much. By cunning they deceive all his possessions and one by one, including his brothers, Draupadi and their Maya palace.

Draupadi feels sorrowful for the loss of Yudhistir. Duryodhana plans to offend Draupadi by pulling her to the justice assembly. When she is brought to the assembly, one in the assembly could save her. Lastly, she turns towards Karna, with bclicf that hc would hclp her. But Karna, to her horrified tells Duryodhan to undress her. That is the first time Draupadi detests Karna. Everyone feels sad and pity for Draupadi. She cursed all those who are assembled there by saying:

All of you will die in the battle that will be spawned from this day's work. Your mothers and wives will weep far more piteously than I have wept. This entire kingdom will become a charnel house. Not one Kaurava heir will be left to offer prayers for the dead. All that will remain is the shameful memory of today, what you tried to do to a defenseless woman - (Divakaruni 194)

Duryodhana remanding the stipulations that they should leave the palace and go on discharge for twelve years. Draupadi decides to go to the forest with her husbands. She leaves her children under the care of Subhadra. When she goes to her palace, her trustful retainers do not want Duryodhana to take control over palace.

So they set fire to the palace. Draupadi feels sad about the loss of the palace. They leave for the forest. Draupadi's husbands are always considerate towards her. But Draupadi whenever she served them always thought of the insult that happened to her in the palace. One day sage Durvas come to their place and ordered them to provide food for him. They feel sad because there is no food, but at this time they are scared that he would get angry. Krishna comes to rescue them, he eats one morsel of rice and that satisfies Durvasa's appetite. The years pass by, Arjun goes to meditate to get powerful weapons from Shiva to fight against Karna. They finish twelve years in exile and in the thirteenth year they go in disguise to King Virat's kingdom. If Duryodhana is able to find them this year, then they should go for another twelve years in exile. In Virat's kingdom, each person plays a different role. Virat's wife is Sudeshna and her brother Keechak. Keechak is attracted towards Draupadi's sake.

Duryodhana comes to know where the Pandavas is hiding there because other than that Pandavas no one could have killed Keechak. Hearing the ideas of Karna, they decide to wage war on Virat's kingdom. So that Pandavas would come before them. But by that time their period of exile will be got over. So Yudhistir will ask Duryodhana to get prepared for the Great War yet to come. They start preparing for the Great War that is going to take place. On Yudhistir's side there are seven kingdoms and Kauravas side there are eleven kingdoms.

Both Arjuna and Duryodhana go to Krishna to support them. But Krishna tells them that he would only act as a charioteer and he would not fight in the war. So Duryodhan decides Krishna's army to be on his side and Arjun wants Krishna to be his charioteer. Before the war starts Draupadi dreamed that Karna is getting blessing from Kundi and she is crying by hugging Karna. Draupadi is confused by the dream. Then Yudhistir shows the place where the war is going to be held to Draupadi, Kunti and Uttara (Abhimanyu's wife).

In the meantime, Indra tricks Karna by coming in the disguise of the poor Brahmin and asks him to give up his armor that is protecting him from his birth. Karna readily gives it all up and this results in his defeat in the war. Draupadi feels sad because Arjun is sure that he would defeat Karna with all his weapons. Though Bheesma, Drona all love Pandavas their promise to Duryodhan made them to support him. When Bheesma is defeated, he is lying in the bed of arrows. Both Pandavas and Kaurava visit him and act according to his advice. When Draupadi comes to visit Bheesma, she sees Karna confessing to Bheesma. Karna tells him that he loved Draupa di from the moment he sees her on her wedding day.

> When Dussasan started pulling at her saree, I could not bear it. I wanted to knock him down, to shield her from the stars. The twelve years she was in forest, I, too, slept on the ground, thinking of her discomfort. How many times I started to go to her, to beg her to come away with me, to be my queen. But I knew it was hopeless. She was completely loyal to her husbands. My words would only disgust her. (Divakaruni 276)

He feels sad for insulting Draupadi in front of others. Karana also tells Bheesma that he is Kunti's son and Kunti has promised to marry him to Draupadi on condition that he should not harm his brothers. Draupadi is shocked when she heard this. She could not believe that Kunti had said these words. She is angry with Kunti for promising such things without her permission. From the next day,

Draupadi watched only Karna. At the moment she hears the words of Karna all her anger towards him vanished. She feels happy that he reciprocates her love.

The following people die in the war-Gadothkacha (Bheema's son), Abhimanyu (Arjuna's son), Bheesma, Drona, all the hundred Kauravas, Karna, all the sons of Pandavas, Sikhandi, Dhristadyumna, Virat, Saguni and Drupada.

After the war gets over, Gandhari and Dhritarashtra are angry toward the Pandavas for killing Kauravas. Krishna advices them that it is their fate and they should not get angry towards Pandavas. Draupadi feels sad about her sons' death. Pandavas feel worried for the death of Karna after they come to know that he is their elder brother. Many women become widows because of the war. Abhimanyu's son Pariks is appointed as the king. Kunti, Gandhari and Dhritarashtra will leave the kingdom and go to the forest and Krishna would be unexpectedly killed by a hunter. Krishna's brother Balaram also would be dead.

The Pandavas also renounces their kingdom and decided to go to the Himalayas. But they will not be able to continue their journey because one by one they will all die on the way. Draupadi would be the first person to fall down. Though Yudhistir knows that Draupadi is in love with Karna he says that she loves Arjuna the most and that is her weakness. He conceals the truth from others. Draupadi thinks of Krishna at this time and he magically appears before her. He advices her and shows her the way to heaven. There she magically appears before her. He advices her and shows her the way to heaven. There she sees everybody, including her brother Dhristadyumna, Duryodhana and Karna.

Karna stretches out his hand and she gladly accepts it. She feels embarrassed to hold hands in front of her husbands, but she realizes that it is heaven and it is free from any bonds of marriage. So, she completes her full circle of her life, only to meet Karna at the very end. She is finally free of all inhibitions and she is free to "take him arm in view of everyone. If I wish I can embrace him with all of myself" (Divakaruni 359). At the End she feels, "I'm truly Panchali. I reach with my other hand, for Karna-how surprisingly solid his clasp! About us our palace waits, the only one I've ever needed".(Divakaruni 360)

Deconstruction is more a practice than a theoretical concept. Through deconstruction, we can focus the novel from Draupadi's point of view, her desire to find true love throughout her life. Through the narrative of the original epic is much different from what is represented by Divakaruni, still the title itself. *The Palace of Illusions* indicates the ultimate barrenness of Draupadi's hearts symbolizing as the palace itself is the creation of Maya. Even her birth is not even wished for. She comes out of the celestial yaga fire with her brother Dhristadyumna for a purpose of taking vengeance against her father oldest enemy Drona. And in her own house, her voice of protest, willingness to learn, taking part in armor activities and even her right to choose her better half are vehemently silenced.

Draupadi is the uttermost complicated and disputed female character in Hindu literature. On the one hand, she could be womanly, generous and sympathetic and on the other hand, she could castigate destroy on those who did her wrong. She was never ready to consolation on either her rights as a daughter-in-law or even on the rights of the Pandavas and remained ever ready to fight back or avenge high- handedness and dishonesty meted out to her submissive. She was secretly subservient that one day she would definitely seek revenge on the injustice meted out to her. She did it by burning the spark of vengeance in the hearts of the Pandavas.

If the Mahabharata is clearly woven sage of hatred and love,courage and cowardice, beauty and gentleness,bloodshed and noble thoughts, victory and defeat, then Draupadi is its glowing and shining jewel, casting the shadow of her classic personality over the epic poem and the all- destruction war it describes.

REFERENCES

- Divakaruni, Chitra Banerjee. *The Palace of Illusions.* New York: Doubleday Broadway Publishing Group, 2008. Print.
- Campbell, Joseph, with Bill Moyers. *The Power of Myth.* New York: Doubleday Dell

  Publishing Group, Inc. 1988. Print.

- Rajagopalachari, C. Preface to second Edition of *Mahabharata.* Bombay: Bharatiya Vidhya Bhavan Limited, 2001. Print.
- Robinson, Herbert Spencer. *Myths and Legends of all Nations.* Totowa, NJ: Little Field,

  Adams & Co, 1976. Print.

- Bhawalkar. V. Eminent. *Women in the Mahabharada,* NewDelhi: Sharda Publishing House,2002. Print.

CHAPTER TWO

Historical And Cultural Labyrinth of The Subcontinent in Gita Hariharan's The Thousand Faces of Night

Colonialism was a global phenomenon and the records of history were to limelight the fact that we had lost our originality.

"Whenever colonization is a fact, the indigenous culture begins to rot. And among the ruins something begins to be born which is not a culture, but a kind of subculture which is condemned to exist on the margin ... a few men, ... who find themselves placed in the most artificial condition, deprived of any reifying contact with the masses of the people." -Aime Cessaire

Colonial India is a part of the Indian Sub-continent, which was under the control of European colonial powers, through trade and conquest. Though India freed herself from the shackles of the British in 1947, it is to be borne in mind that association between these two nations had been for nearly three hundred and fifty years, and as far as the socio-political consciousness of India is concerned these years are to be termed as crucial years in Indian history. It is true that the impact of the still colonial culture is being felt and experienced in decolonized societies. Consequently, the larger portion of post colonial India has internalized the culture and values of the west, which reflect on the image of Eurocentricism. A vast majority of Postcolonial writing recovery them of the self and the native culture from the dominance of the colonizer.Thus, both modernism and colonies, though from a different historical background, theories and motivations have some aspects in common. The second generation Indian English fiction can comfortably be viewed under four different aspects: Feminist discourse, Ethno-religious or Minority discourse, Diaspora discourse and political/ideological discourse. Feminism has become one of the most far-reaching movements this world has witnessed. Its influence has been felt in every area of social, political and cultural life worldwide. Indeed, feminism has achieved the dubious distinction of becoming a familiar part of our cultural landscape. The work of Indian women writers is significant in making society aware of women's demands, and in providing a medium for self-expression and re-writing the history of India. Githa Hariharan , with such craftsmanship and the sensibility of the creative artist, has attempted the exposure of the cultural conglomeration and conflict through her works. Many of her works has aptly portrayed the encounter between the East and West.

Githa Hariharan was born in 1954 in Coimbatore, India, to a Tamil Brahmin Family, from Palghat, South India. Her father was a journalist with a renowned Indian newspaper –the Times of India. Her mother a homemaker dedicated her life in the upbringing of her three children. Blessed with a happy childhood, Hariharan as a child enjoyed full liberty in the dizzying company of books. Having fed with the richness of Victorian classics and the Japanese novels, Hariharan's upbring was not liberal, not oppressive. She grew up in Bombay and Manila. She received her education both in India and in the United States. A personage of versatility, she has tried her hands in varied arenas. She has served as a staff editor in WNET – Channel 13 in New York, and from 1979, she served in Bombay, Madras and New Delhi as an editor, first in a publishing house, then as a freelancer. Githa Hariharan is a social reformist and nationalist to the core. She engages herself in reforming the ills of our society. Thus, in 1995, Hariharan questioned the validity of the Hindu Minority and Guardianship Act as they are discriminatory against women. The case, "Githe Hariharan and another Vs. Reserve Bank of India", paved the way for a Supreme Court judgment in 1999 on guardianship. She has carved a niche for herself as a well-acclaimed writer. Her published works comprise novels, essays, short stories, newspaper articles and columns. Her first novel, The Thousand Faces of Night (1992) won the Commonwealth Writer Prize in 1993. Her other novels include The Ghosts of Vasu Master (1994), When Dreams Travel (1999), In Times of Siege (2003), and the latest Fugitive Histories (2009). She is also the author of a collection of highly acclaimed short stories, The Art of Dying, which was published in 1993. She also published a book of stories for children, 'The Winning Team' in 2004. She has edited a volume of stories in English translation from fine major South Indian Languages, 'A southern harvest'. Moreover, a collection of stories for children, 'Sorry Best friend' (1997) has been co-edited by her. Hariharan's name and fame attained international status, that her works, in particular, her fiction has been translated into a number of languages, namely Spanish, German, French, Dutch, Greek, Urdu, Italian, and Vietnamese. Again in anthologies such as Salman Rushdie's Mirror Work: 50 years of Indian Writing; 1947-1997, her essays and fiction have been included. She regularly writes a column for the major Indian Newspaper 'The Telegraph'.

Hariharan as a Visiting Professor has been visiting several Universities namely George Washington University in the United States, the University of Canterbury at Kent in the UK, Dartnorth College and James Miller Islamia in India. As a gifted writer, Hariharan, with her creative craftsmanship delves into the secrets of life and lays bare its realities. Widely renowned for her social consciousness, critical analysis and realistic appreciation, she aspires to explore the appalling plight of the fairer sex in all fields of life-social, economical, political, cultural, this in fact has elevated her literary venture.

Hariharn's first novel The thousand faces of the night (1992), highlights the survival strategies of women belonging to three different generations. The novel has won the Commonwealth Prize for the First best book. The protagonist of the novel, Devi, being the youngest of the three, is the US-return modern woman who ends up in a bitter marriage. Another powerful character in the novel is her mother Sita, who strives for her self–assertion by aspiring to bridge the widening gap between tradition and modernity. Mayamma, being the last, is the old family retainer in Devi's husband's house, and is a real typical instance of women's exploitation by patriarchal society. She belongs to the distant past with her affixed location in the suffocating tradition and whose pathetic life displays that for an Indian woman Married life becomes a success only if she endures all the torture heaped on her without retort. Hariharan's portrayal of this relationship clearly reflects her notions about the plight of wives in India. The primary thing that strikes is the insensitivity of Indian husbands to the psychology of their wives. Even the educated husbands like Mahesh, who is representing the whole educated male chauvinistic.

Within the vast family of Indian writers in English Githa Hariharan's works mirror the historical repercussions both at the personal and public level. Literature is a manifestation of the cultural ,social, political and spiritual growth of a nation. Literature is a mirror of society because it personifies not only the long cherished and the deep rooted traditional, but also a comprehensive perception of the changing aspects of society with contemporary life and true reality of a nation. To understand the customs and cultural modes of a nation, one should study thematic concerns and innovative writing techniques like the tools Hariharan adopts are quite sharp and probe very deep. She has skillfully done the orchestration of innumerable stories. The central theme and around with social evils, historical romance, social realism, hunger, poverty, tradition versus modernity are found in the literary works of earlier periods in Indian writing in English like culture, feminism. Our life is in great flux. Movement like Communism, Socialism, Feminism and Humanism like waves in the sea came one after the other and brought change after change in this present society. Hariharan is perhaps the Indian author who has made a bold attempt to give voice to the frustrations and disappointments of women despite her vehement denial of being feminist. She is a best passport to be called an articulator of the whole woman's society who are caught at the crossroads of change in a society which is undergoing the birth pangs of transition from tradition to the present modernity.

Gita Hariharan has dealt with serious thoughts on the females' pathetic condition in Indian society, superstitions, myths, religion, marriage and love. Her novel Thousand Faces of Night presents the effects of patriarchy on women of different social classes and ages and particularly the varied responses to the restrictive institution of marriage. However, a peep into ancient times seems to reveal interesting facts about women's status. Women enjoyed a much advanced status, where matriarchy was the rule. It is believed that the family of early humans centered around the mother. Prior status was given to female deities. A patriarchal social set up firmly asserts men's superiority over women and is based not on mutuality, but on oppression. Although, women have played a crucial role in the creation of society and have been active agents in history, yet the patriarchal thought has spared no effort to relegate them to the margins equal status was endowed upon women to participate in sacrificial rites on par with men during the Vedic period. They enjoyed the privileges of fighting wars, involving themselves in philosophical debates and were allowed to hold on to their spinstership if they so desired.

Women are worthy of worship. They are the fate of the household, the lamp of enlightenment for all in the household. They bring solace to the family and are an integral part of dharmic life. Even heaven is under the control of women. The gods reside in those households where women are worshipped and in households where women are slighted all efforts at improvement go in vain. Manusmriti 3-56

Unlike in the ancient Indian period, the position and status of women in the Mughal period were not prurliged. Polygamy and child marriage had become common. While the birth of a daughter was considered to be inauspicious, that of a son was an occasion for rejoicing. On account of early marriage, there were many widows in our society. Generally, women in Mughal Period were not allowed to remarry. Rig Veda clearly approves of remarriage of a widow. Such women faced no condemnation or isolation in the household or society. They had the right to property inherited from their dead husbands. Sati as a practice is described as a Hindu custom in India. . It is also imperative to comprehend the cultural background of Indian Women through the ages to assess the plight of Indian women in the backdrop of the wide canvass of Indian women of different ages. It is interesting to note that an elevated status has been awarded to them in Indian religion and philosophical thought.

Hariharn's first novel The thousand faces of night (1992), Which has won the Commonwealth Prize for the First best book. Highlights the survival strategies of women belonging to three different generations.The protagonist of the novel, Devi, being the youngest of the three, who has returned from the US and is trapped in a bitter marriage. Devi thus in her frantic attempts to be an ideal wife and daughter-in-law Devi gradually loses her individuality. She lives like a stranger in her own home. Man and woman need each other's love for maintaining a harmony in their physical and mental health. But all her attempts are neither appreciated nor recognized by Mahesh. Her husband always on tours, remains a shadowy stranger, who views marriage as just another necessity. Gradually Devi discovers the fact that Mahesh can neither accept nor recognized her efforts in love, in fact, he scorns at her education whenever a wordy argument arises between them Mahesh uttered, "This is what comes of educating a woman. Your grandmother was barely illiterate. Wasn't she a happy woman than you are? " Devi feels that her education has not prepared is defenseless against Mahesh's supreme confidence and superciliousness. Mahesh never takes any initiative to spend adequate time with Devi Thus, it clearly indicates that a male chauvinist like Mahesh could never think of their better-half to be on par with them. The sole motive of marriage for him was to produce a baby and a Devi was the means to the fulfilment of his motive. Her urge for a strong sense of revenge is manifested in different forms. She identifies herself with Durga, the goddess who is the destroyer of evil. She says, " I lived a life of my own. I become a woman warrior, a heroine. I was Devi. I rode a tiger, and cut off evil, magical demon's heads" Thus the old and the outworn order has to be destroyed giving place to a new one. Devi had an extramarital with Gopal, a musician. Condemning Mahesh to a lonely life. She went away with Gopal hoping to find her own emotional voice through music.

She realizes Gopal is also cannot see beyond either the passion of music. The fascination of the new relationship comes to end in her own realization. The two choices Devi has made result in nonfulfillment. While leaving Mahesh she felt bold as a heroine. Now she is not on the run, but she feels like a fugitive escaping from captivity to a stage of self-recognition. Her final union with her mother can be seen as frantic attempts of an alienated woman trying to seek a heaven of shelter and security. Devi represents the present-day intellectual woman, who confronts loneliness and alienation However, some of the incidents of her life are very close to day to day reality. Her problems are just what we have seen around us. Thus the novel reflects the continuing and inherent tension between the reinforcing of traditions and the resistance to recurrent cultural patterns. Hariharan seems to attribute such arrogance of Mahesh to the embedded conceptions about a woman's role in the Indian male psyche and women's powerlessness to the dominant mentalities of India. She negotiates the feminism issues across various contradictions of our country. Another powerful character in the novel is her mother Sita, who strives for herself assertion by aspiring to bridge the widening gap between tradition and modernity. Mayamma, being the last, is the old family retainer in Devi's husband's house, and is a real typical instance of women's exploitation by patriarchal society. She belongs to the distant past with her affixed location in the suffocating tradition and whose pathetic life displays that for an Indian woman Married life becomes a success only if she endures all the torture heaped on her without retort. Hariharan through this novel, which is in fact a collage-like, work, records her deep sense of anguish against the Indian patriarchal ideologies that subjugate women to the core .Phrases like 'Virtuous lady '. 'Ideal wife, Ideal daughter-in-law' in fact are devices propagated by the patriarchal structure to subjugate women. From yonder years till the present day, these ideologies have been passed on, that even elite, educated men adhere to them seriously and fail to consider that a woman is indeed an individual human with all other emotions and feelings. It is true that the novels of the post-colonial age emphasizes on a quest for identity along a different dimension of the socio-political and economic order of India. This novel emphasizes the themes of gender and identity. It is to be noted that it is the identity that marks the convolutions and collusions of external and internal, individual and collective, natural and cultural forces. Analyzing 'gender identity' in a broader perspective, one can seen that gender interacts with other markers of identity – religion, ethnicity, national and familiarity. Githa Hariharan's attempts to unleash the different degrees of adjustments, opposition, resistance and struggle, of her women characters, help her reflect out the lack of flexibility in patterns of social organization and the high levels of frustration and suffering experienced by women. Through her works, She has succeeded in putting forth certain definite reforms that can be initiated to uplift the aspirations of women. Our epics, Vedas and Puranas envisage marriage not as a mere social instrument but also as a moral weapon to both stabilize and elevate the moral stature of an individual. But unfortunately, it is an irony of fate that in a post- modernistic world, such esteemed institutions are currently subject to doubt.

An Existential Crisis is slowly coming to the conclusion through representing self-actualization as an identity. We each need to find meaning in their lives. Meaning is found through interpersonal relationships. This is also pointed out by the brilliant psychiatrist and psychotherapist, Irvin Yalom, MD. The stories of three different women separate yet linked, are knit together. The novel is woven around three generations of women Devi, Sita and Mayamma. It presents how the female point of view differs from the male discourse, especially in marriage. The psychological differences between man and women are less obvious. They can be difficult to describe. Yet these differences can profoundly influence how we form and maintain relationships that can range from work and friendships to marriage and parenting. There is evidence to suggest that a great deal of the sensitivity that exists within men and women has a physiological basis. Many people fail to realize that they have an enormous influence on the lives of others. Whether they are friends or family, they are important to us and we are important to them. There are also the relationships with those at work and those we casually meet while walking in the street, riding the bus or train, and shopping in the supermarket and clothing store. it is also important to know that each of us is unique and individual. As John Donne said it centuries ago:

No man is an island, entire of itself...any man's death diminishes me, because I am involved in mankind; and therefore never send to know for whom the bell tolls; it tolls for thee.

Donne was meaning three things: That none of us are isolated because we are all interconnected, We are all aware of death and One man's death diminishes all mankind. On the whole, all these female based stories longing for real love from their dear once when it fails, they come to a conclusion towards self actualization even though they are dependent on one another out of their life partner. Devi and her mother rejoined to rejoice in their own life in their own way. Mayamma spent her life after her own family passed away to take care Parvatiamma's family. Parvatiamma devoted herself towards the love of the almighty and self actualisation. Githa Hariharan's attempts to unleash the different degrees of adjustments, opposition, resistance and struggle, of her women characters, and thereby she points out the lack of flexibility in patterns of social organization and the high levels of frustration and suffering experienced by women. She has succeeded in putting forth through her works certain definite reforms that can be initiated to uplift the aspirations of women.As women were oppressed by this system, their consciousness to fight for their rights and break the system of patriarchy gradually arises. This awakening usually linked by the women movement called feminism. We are constantly developing our identity, from birth to the end of our lives. Various groups have been formed to give women's history a voice, to promote the study of women's history and to maintain links with contemporary feminist activists. Hariharan perception envelops the whole history of woman's role and uplifts the emergence of a new woman who is true to her own self and quest for self actualization. The protagonist Devi Sandwiched between tradition and modernity, illusion and reality and the mask and the face, she led a life of restlessness. Reality is situated in the individual subjective consciousness. The inability to communicate one's inner experiences is to other leads to self imposed alienation or isolation from society. All the three main female characters progress to delimiting restrictions through self analysis and self discovery, they try to create both physical as well as psychological space for themselves to grow on their own. She explains the human relationship in modern Indian society, particularly the husband wife relationship elaborated clearly from their personal point of view. Her women characters are entirely tolerant, obedient and submissive.The major them of this work running throughout is one closely to the psychological crisis, Loss of identity and the way it travels through generation to generation as a sense of loss.

Whereas the average individuals "often have not the slightest idea of what they are, of what they want, of what their own opinions are," self-actualizing individuals have "superior awareness of their own impulses, desires, opinions, and subjective reactions in general.

~ Abraham Maslow Quotes from Motivation & Personality

As the above quote said superior awareness of Devi' quest is to regain her lost identity and to be truthful to her desires by gaining control over her true 'self'. Human life has been viewed both as a journey as well as a battle. The journey charts out the progression, the movement from womb to tomb and even beyond. The story contains within its fold manifold dreams so many sub stories interlinked to the main fold, desires, expectations, aspirations as well as frustrations and embitterment. Self-actualization is not just about knowing and fulfilling one's purpose in life. Knowing that you have fulfilled a purpose in life is what creates us to feel worthy, happy, and content with our own life. Individuals who are lost and depressed do not feel a sense of worthiness in their lives; thus, they must seek and desire self-actualization to be met in order to gain the identity like protagonist Devi finds her identity at lost by union with her mother it helps her to feel life is not stopping with Mahesh or Gopal and she wants to achieve to prove her life note worth. Reaching this level of Maslow's hierarchy of needs is what fulfills the most happiness and content feeling of one's life. Surpassing the needs of physiology, safety, belongingness, and esteem, build up all together in self-actualization. Reaching the top of Maslow's pyramid is the source of happiness. The loss of self identity in a woman is the root cause of many conflicts; a promising search for selfhood is essential for all-round happiness. But Devi is confident of her capabilities to make choices and assumes control over her life. The courage, the dignity, the responsibility and the independent spirit displayed by her proves that she is reached a stage of self actualization. She proves that women like her are capable of ushering in a positive change in the social structure.

Gita Hariharan vision encompasses the whole history of woman's role in the cultural labyrinth and edifies the emergence of a new woman who is true to her own self. All the three women in the novel tried from their utmost level to brave, the strong oppositions and design a room of their own. This awakening is usually linked by the women's movement called feminism. We are constantly developing our identity, from birth to the end of our lives. Various groups have been formed to give women's history a voice, to promote the study of women's history and to maintain links with contemporary feminist activists. In 1991 leading women historians came together to launch the Women's History Network (WHN) The International Federation for Research in Women's History (IFRWH), established in 1987, has similar aims and encourages co-operation across national boundaries.

REFERENCES

Hariharan,Gita. *The Thousand Faces of Night*, New Delhi: Penguin books India, 1992.Print.

Dodiya, Jaydipsinh. *Indian Women Novelists in English.* New Delhi: Sarup & Sons, 2006. Print.

Rahman, Gulrez Roshan *Indian Writing in English: New Critical Perspectives.*New Delhi: Sarup Book Pvt.Ltd., 2012. Print.

Prasad, Amar Nath. New Lights on Indian Women Novelists in English.New Delhi: Sarup & Sons, 2005. Print.

Bhargava, Rajul. *Indian Writing in English: The Last Decade.* New Delhi : Rawat Publications,2002.Print.

Howatson, M.C. and Lan Chilvers. *Oxford Concise Companion to Classical Literature*. New York : Oxford University Press,1993.Print.

Indira, S. 1994. "*Walking the Tight Rope : A Reading of Githa Hariharan's The Thousand Faces of Night*". *Fiction of the Nineties*. New Delhi: Prestige Books,1994.Print.

Shahane, V.A. Introduction: Explorations in Modern Indo-English Fiction. Ed. R.K.Dhawan. New Delhi: Classical Publishing Company,1982. Print.

Guha, Ramachandra. India after Gandhi: The History of the world's largest Democracy. London: Pan Macmillan,2008.Print.

CHAPTER THREE

Culture Conflicts in Rajam Krishnan's Lamps in The Whirlpool

Rajam Krishnan was born in 1925 in *Musiri, Trichy* District in Tamil Nadu. She is a famous Tamil writer. Her works depict the lives of women in Tamil Nadu, particularly the Brahmin women, in a realist style and lucid language. The intertwining of tradition and modernity is one of the hallmarks of her writing. She is unable to come to terms with what she perceives to be the unchanging plight of women in society, irrespective of whether they are traditional or modern. She once remarked in an interview "It is a shame that the suffering women underwent in my days dog them even now". *RajamKrishnan*'s works express her anguish at the way inequities are perpetuated in one form after another. Her novels and short stories have been translated into various Indian languages and English. *Rajam* was left poor and destitute in her later years and had to bead mitted to an old age home. She died on 20 October

2014. She is a recipient of the NewYork Herald Tribune International Award in 1950 for a short story; *Sahitya AkademiAward in 1973*; *Soviet Land Nehru Award* in 1975. She has been honoured with several other awards such as Kalaimagal Award in 1953 and *Thiru.Vi.Ka. Award* in 1991.She started publishing in her twenties. She is known for writing well researched social novels on the lives of people usually not depicted in modern Tamilliterature - poor farmers, salt pan workers, small time criminals, jungle dacoits, under-trial prisoners, and female laborers. She has written more than 80 books. Her works include forty novels, twenty plays, two biographies and several short stories. In additi onto her own writing, she was a translator of literature from Malayalam to Tamil. In the anthology of Women's writing in India in 19th and 20th Century, Susie J Tharu and K. Lalita credit Krishnan with "having set a new trend in Tamil literature," referring to the extensive research that Krishnan did in evaluating social conditions as back ground for her writing. Her popular Tamil novels are *KurinjiThen (1963), Valaikaram (1969), Verukku Neer, Malargal (1974), MullumMalarndhadhu (1974), Paadaiyil Padinda Adigal (1991),Alaivaaikarayile (1978),Karippu Manigal (1979), Mannakattu puntulikal (1988),Suzhalil Mithakkum Deepangal(Lamps in the Whirlpool) (1995). New York Herald Tribune International Award for ashort story (1950), Kalaimagal Award (1953), Sahitya Akademi Award for Tamil for Verukku Neer (Water for the Roots) (1973), Thiru.Vi.Ka Award (1991) Malargal(Flowers) (1974), Ananda Vikatan Novel Prize Winner (1958), Soviet LandNehru Award (1975) for Valaikkaram (Wrist with Bangles).*

Lamps in the Whirlpool written by *Rajam Krishnan* is a translation of the *Suzhalil Mithakkum Deepangal.* The *"lamps"* in the title symbolize the situation of women in the family as the whirlpool indicates the inconvenience that is faced by women. Specifically, the author gives a description of feminism and orthodox regulations of the Brahmin community in this novel. She gives an emphasis to "madi rules and Brahmin women are endured by that "madi rules". The central character, Girija moves violently in an orthodox Brahmin family to maintain her authority in her home and she comes out by violating the convention in the orthodox parameter. And the mutual understanding between *Girija* and her husband Swaminathan.The protagonist *Girija* is a middle-class girl, post-graduated and has served in a

village school for eight years and she got married to Swaminathan who is qualified and well placed in life. After marriage, she does not want to go for a job. After bearing two daughters and a son and serving her mother-in-law with uncompromising devotion for seventeen years observing strict rules of "madi". Girija comes to realize the emptiness of her life and the insidious exploitation of her natural docility and goodness by the mother and son. She becomes aware of it by the talk of "consciousness raising" by *Ratna,* her husband's niece, who is a chance to visit. After a long tour, Swaminathan drops in only to pack up and leave on yet another profession trip. He is insensitive to his wife's state of mind. Losing his temper and

male egoistic, anger he shows his crude behavior toward her. His mother does not seem to think that her son was either unreasonable or boorish. So, she takes the decision of leaving the family. She spends four days in Haridwar and feels enlightened and returns home. The mother-in-law and her husband charge her within infidelity and order her to clear out of the house. She is horrified by their cruel assumptions. Girija goes out in search of *Ratna*. Understanding *Girija*'s predicament, *Ratna* and her friends in the hostel give her temporary refuge and take care of her. She seeks employment with a nun who is running a home for refugee children. Her concern is to see her daughters, when they are grown up, are not destroyed by the family regimen. The woman who is the linchpin of the family, who effaces herself as a person so that she may be a wife, mother, daughter-in-law, most of all. *Virginia Woolf* long ago wrote in professions for Women about the Angel in the House, She was intensely charming. She was utterly unselfish. She excelled in the difficult arts of family life. She sacrificed herself daily. If there was chicken, she took the leg; if there was a draught she sat in it- in short, she was so constituted that she never had a mind or wish of her own, but preferred to sympathize always with the minds and wishes of others. The Indian woman in the family is worshipped as an angel if she annihilates herself for the sake of others. She is suitably married off to perform the duties of a Hindu wife in a Brahmin community. She has been trained to regard being a dutiful wife and daughter-in-law as the only goal of a woman's life. She is given in marriage to *Swaminathan.* His mother symbolizes the cruelty that Indian woman perpetrates on womanhood, having chosen *Girija* as a daughter-in-law calculates the prospect of her becoming a thoroughly obedient person. On the eve of the marriage, she presents *Girija* with a pair of diamond earrings and a pair of nose studs. Such generosity is rare and *Girija's* mother and brother are deeply impressed. They do not expect anything to go wrong in Girija's life. The women become representative of societal rituals, customs and traditions. *Girija* has to

practice ritual purity, referred as madi. She is subject to several restrictions such as repeated baths and fasting while cooking meals for her elderly widowed mother-in-law. The concept of purity and pollution is firmly reinforced through the practice of madi, which had to be solely practiced by her. Her husband and son were excluded from such rituals. Girija's mother-in-law through a façade of powerlessness, and ritual purity, exercises her power and authority over the lives of her son and daughter-in-law and disrupts their domestic harmony. Her physical and mental stress is not considered, due respect is not provided and priority is not given by her and by her family members at any instance. *Girija* faces inconvenience because of her mother-in-law: *Kavi* and *Charu* ran naked like slum children. If they wore clothes and
touched her, she had to bathe again before cooking! She had been so ashamed of their appearances, especially when friends and students visited her. Many people have an education, but they do not question the traditions and culture of their ancestors. Particularly, in general, women are compelled to follow the rituals. In every community women are expected to follow the rituals and customs. Being a postgraduate woman is forced to follow *madi* rules by her mother-in-law. According to the *madi* rules, a wife should take an early bath before entering the kitchen. She must wash her night clothes daily. Particularly, widows must wear "*narmadi*". *Girija* follows this *madi* rules, without any objection as per her mother-in-
law's order. *Girija* does not like those rules, even though she follows it at the instance of her mother-in-law. Nevertheless, her mother-in-law does not help *Girija* in any way. Instead of that, she remains free from all her responsibilities. Her foremost job is to supervise her

daughter-in-law. *Swaminathan* pays his attention only to his business. He does not show any kind of support or love or affection for her. He denies staying or listening to her words and pretends as if he is busy with his work. *Girija* is always entangled with her household work and runs like a machine without ego. She feels that everything is sacrificed only for the sake of her husband and children's welfare. Though an educated woman, she is an equally foolish woman who sacrifices her life for domestic harmony. *Girija* allowed herself to be treated like a worm and worked like a machine. She realizes her state of ignorance only when *Ratna* makes it clear that a single note, however melodious, does not create harmony. *Girija*, being the single note, is not a real zest in the family. It is nothing but exploitation. Bernard Shaw comments on the relationship between a husband and a wife as follows:

Man and wife do not, as a rule, live together; they only breakfast together, dine together and sleep in the same room. In most cases the women know nothing of the man's working life and he knows nothing of her working life [He calls it her home life].

From this point of view, husband and wife both should mutually understand and share their views and feelings such as: good and bad, development of the family, the financial status of the home, and children's education with them. They should be given self-respect to each other more than love. If it happens so then their life would be filled and continued with the stream of love forever. But here, *Girija* lost her identity and self-respect from their family members. Her sense of right and wrong find a voice through *Ratna*. The wrongs done to women in the name of madi have extremely impaired her.

Ratna tells Girija:

What a disgrace! They treat you like a worm and make you work like a machine. Harmony is achieved only when all the noted are in perfect accord. A single note, however melodious, does not create harmony (12).

According to the above quote, Girija's husband, on the other hand, considers her as a worm destined to serve him and his mother. But in all fairness, he had no bad habits, he did not drink or smoke, nor was he interested in other women. There had been no secrets between them. He was authoritative by nature. She had always given to him. Girija's husband always went on business trips, when he returned from the trips with a pile of dirty clothes and it was her responsibility to get them washed and pressed. She took care of him in each and every detail, but Swaminathan did not like her that much. Every woman wanted to be taken care of by her husband during her time of illness. Girija also felt like that, but her husband did not bother about it. He feels that she was a machine to do all the household work without fail. She did not have the right to ask a simple question to him, she had not even raised her voice against him. She was dazed at her husband's unkindness towards her when she enquired about a small briefcase. She was totally disillusioned and disturbed. An uncontrollable urge and an inexplicable desire have impelled *Girija* to leave home. Bednar described as follows,

A home with a loving and loyal husband and wife is the supreme setting in which children can be reared in love and righteousness

> and in which
> the spiritual and physical needs of children can be met (http://mobile.brainyquote.com).

From this, the home can make by a loving husband and wife. They are the role model for their children and they have to mould them on the right path in which physical and spiritual way. *Girija* has torn herself away from her family with the implicit faith that she would find peace on the banks of the Ganges. Without giving prior information to anyone she steps out of her home to find some relief on the banks of the Ganga and reach Rishikesh Ashram. Before her departure from her home, she removes her ,diamond ring, earring and nose ring that removal which is symbolized as the bondage of slavery . Moreover, Girija removes her thali instead of that she wears a chain because it was bought out of her own earnings. Girija leaves her home to seek some relief on the banks of the Ganga. She meets an elderly pilgrim couple and stays with them while in Haridwar. Jack Kingston explains about the relationship between husband and wife is,

> Ages of experience have taught humanity that the commitment of a husband and wife to love and to serve one another promotes the welfare of children and the stability of society (http://mobile.brainyquote.com).

In that, he clearly tells about the duties of a husband and wife for society. She finds that the old woman Gowri Ammal has been treated abominably by her arrogant husband who was a Munsiff. But in old age, the woman talks of her past without any bitterness and ironically, now, her husband totally dependent on her. Girija also meets a spiritual widow in Rishikesh who recounts her life of misery as the third wife to an elderly man and the tale of tyranny of her stepson who was a menace to her youth. That woman finally dared to defy society after her husband's death by drowning while on a pilgrimage and choose to stay in the „Ashram"(52) at Rishikesh, helping a young one in his medical rounds in the neighborhood as an Ayurvedic healer. *Girija* explains her situation to the woman. She advises *Girija* to take life in her hands and act with clarity. She returns home with a sense of enlightenment, after four days.

Girija's husband and mother-in-law lay the blame on her with disloyalty and command her to leave the house. When she returns home, her entry is barred, for she has the mother-in-law, she is a woman, of course, who is unsympathetic, and that is the greater tragedy of the Indian scene. She is horrified by their cruel assumptions. What pains her more deeply is that Swaminathan tells his son Bharat that *Girija* is a loose woman and has run away. The old lady encourages her son: "The milk is spilt and nothing can be done about it. Let she take her belongings and leave" (61). Girija had received a good education and had even worked for a while. But marriage had caged her. The tragic thing about it is, it can alienate the daughter from father and mother, daughter-in-law from parents-in-law and even from her own children. It can vitiate human relationships when primacy is given to external observances to the petrifaction of the spirit. Further, it can also be a source of much hypocrisy is tellingly portrayed in the character of *Roja Mami*, a friend of the mother-in-law. Claiming to be more than a daughter through log contact, *Roja Mami* exploits the doggedness of the old woman for madi to kindle suspicion leading to inhumanity in the mother-in-law towards the helpless daughter-in-law. *Girija* discovers to her horror after her escape at Haridwar that all that glitters is not gold. Roja Mami and her husband for all their performance of worship to the pontiff camping at Haridwar, are really social culprits, amassing money and treasures illegally, hoarding part of them in her husband's steel wardrobe. Swaminathan refuses to disclose the truth of the antique box lurking in his bureau to *Girija.* His ties with *Roja Mami* seem to be more important than those with his wife. *Roja Mami* has no business to interfere in *Girija's* family affairs and set her husband and mother-in-law against her, pretending to preserve their madi and "aacharam". *Girija* in sheer rage lashes out at her:

> You sanctimonious hag!! Your madi and vizhuppu are all sham, you
> smuggled gold, diamonds, evade taxes and use an ignorant old woman's
> house to stash away your ill-gotten gains. I do not want my children to
> become hypocrites observing hollow madi rituals (64).

Of course, such a denunciation shocks the husband and mother-in-law. But "with her flashing diamonds, outsized pottu, dyed black hair and gaudy silks" (64),

an the appearance which sets off waves of revulsion in *Girija, Roja Mami* lies through her teeth that she did not see *Girija* at Haridwar though in all probability she did sight *Girija* in the crowd thronging around the Swamigal while offering obeisance to him. *Roja Mami* lies in order to slander and malign an innocent woman. It is a pity that the old woman cares more for *Roja Mami's* offended self-respect than for her honest *daughter-in-law's* feelings simply because she believes *Roja Mami* is strict in the observance of madi and that therefore her integrity. Through *Girija,* both when she punctiliously observes the ritual cleanliness in serving her mother-in-law and when she is aghast at being ostracized, the author castigates the system of madi and its observances and their allied virtues. *Rajam Krishnan*, to be sure, is not promoting subversion of the institution of the family for the sake of revolt but she uses it as a shock-treatment to impel us to think about the essentials of human relationships. Crusted over by custom, debilitated by rituals like madi, our present-day family is a far cry from its ideal. The Indian women have no self-identity at all. They lose their self-identity after the marriage ceremony. They are converted into sacrificial goats in the formal procedure of administrating the family. *Girija* is forced to choose between a crushing orthodoxy at home and the freedom of self-expression outside it. Though Mulk Raj Anand advocates the liberation of women, he seems to stress the need to strike a balance to retrain the traditional aspect of life as well. Set in the traditional milieu of this novel also reveal explicit gender dynamics. These characters indicate a cultural situation in which the woman is reduced to the position of the other and forced to live in submission. The hold of the traditional concept of a woman (going back to the Sita- Savitri myth) on the Indian psyche and the attempts of an egotistic patriarchal society to maintain it and keep the woman under control are brought here. The mother-in-law as a woman themselves often indirectly helps in sustaining and nurturing the male social standards. There is a break from the social order, but this is often temporary. The character ends up being conditioned by the society surrounding them or are forced to leave it. The orthodox social setup fiercely resists any deviation from its existing order and one is left to lurch in the darkness. The rebellion is at times feeble and in vain and the outsider ceases to be one because of his feeble attempts. Girija is disgusted and goes to Ratna, who is affianced in feminist studies at Delhi University Ratna is naturally looked upon as the very devil sowing the seeds of discord in an otherwise peaceful family. On the other hand, the author tries to explore, how an ignored child gets into the wrong path. Krishnan introduced a character named Runo, who is ignored by her parents. She lost her mother and father married another lady. So, no one is either to question or answer to her. In this case, she becomes a drug addict and a drunkard. At last, she commits suicide because of her boyfriend who cheated on her.

The implication is the question on how the Indian woman should learn to strike a balance between two extremes. The word Mamiyar symbolizes authority which is often associated with inhumanity. The sight of her mother-in-law in widow's weeds and tonsured head only evokes pity in Girija's mind. Girija has compassion. She is even willing to extenuate the harshness of her mother-in-law on account of her ignorance. Ratna and her friends give her a place of safety and take concern of her as if she were an offended bird. The old woman goes over to the hostel to hand over Girija's certificates and clothes but not her jewelry. Girija is provoked by a cheque for Rs.10,000/- which Swaminathan sends through his mother. Girija flings it back, later she learns that her husband had also come up to the building but had preferred to stay in the car. She is now certain that there is no love between them. Girija looks for employment with a nun who runs a home for expatriate children. Her apprehension now is to see that her daughters are not ruined by the family routine at her own cost. Girija resolves that she will keep in touch with her daughters and train their sensibility in a balanced way, giving them freedom while helping them to develop a sense of self-reliance and responsibility. Thus the author beautifully portrays Girija and her like who assert their individuality are but lamps in the whirlpool of a caste- and custom-ridden society. But as long as there is life, there is hope. Annie advises Girija to accept the job for the time being and appreciates her. "Very good, Girija, you have taken a great stride forward you have discarded some of our ugly customs" (72). Men and women are equal and should be given mutual respect. Lamps in the Whirlpool unquestionably represent the life of women in the contemporary age of *Rajam Krishnan*. Women had no right to express their thoughts or feelings during that period. But now that condition has drastically changed. Women have the same feelings as same as men like love, passion, friendship, and so on. Always a woman sacrifices her life for others. For instance, in her childhood, she lives for her parents, in her later life, she lives for her husband and children and in her old age, she lives for her grandchildren. Girija and Swaminathan have come from the same culture, tradition, religion, and caste. In their life, there is no love and affection. Mutual understanding is missing between them. So life can be complete only with the mutual understanding of the husband and wife. Without a man or woman, life cannot be concluded in a successful way, because man and woman are two parts of the same soul. Along with love and mutual understanding, the family members should follow their customs and tradition. Without culture and tradition, a man's life cannot be fulfilled in society. Mandy Ross says about „Women"s rights", it means making sure that women can take their part in society, use their skills, and fulfill their potential. The struggle is not only to achieve equal treatment for men and women but to recognize the value of women and what they do, as well as to overcome barriers to equality at work and in politics. This battle is not complete, and in some parts of the world women's lives are very far from equal. (The Changing Role of Women, 5).

Rajam Krishnan's Lamps in the Whirlpool, and Lalithambika Antharjanam's Agnisaakshi help to bring out the plight of women caught in the coils of an orthodox social set-up. It helps to lay bare the restrictions imposed by the extremely ritualistic religious practices among the caste of Hindus. The Indian woman is depicted as being held back by the dictates of her husband, parents and brothers, who maintain that she keeps up the Sita-Savitri image. Women in R.K.Narayan's novels like Savitri in The Dark Room and Susila in The English Teacher are generally relegated to the house where innumerable customs and traditions are thrust on them. One also finds that as the social milieu gradually changes, from orthodox one to one of progress and liberation, the women also slowly begin to assert their independence. A number of novelists have portrayed this struggle of a woman against the pretentious pieties of a family, individual or community. Rajam Krishnan, an excellent writer is known for writing social novels on

The lives of people, such as poor farmers, salt workers, and female workers and so on. In this novel, Lamps in the Whirlpool she gives an account of female experiences in the orthodox Brahmin community. It reveals Girija's struggles in an orthodox Brahmin family to maintain her authority in her home and the way she breaks the conventions in the orthodox setup. Girija's mother-in-law and her husband treatedher like a slave, after recognizing herself she leaves from the home and decided her life as she wants. Cultural conflicts are difficult to resolve as parties to the conflict have different beliefs. Cultural conflicts intensify when those differences become reflected in politics, particularly on a macro level. Ethnic cleansing is another extreme example of cultural conflict. Wars can also be a result of a cultural conflict; for example the differing views on slavery were one of the reasons for the American civil war. Girija and Swaminathan belong to the same community and culture. But their way of understanding of life is different. There is no mutual understanding between them. They always had a clash between them according to their culture, traditional and custom. Self is also seen to be the core of all age groups of girls and women and thus life stage approach has been used to analyze it. To begin with, the development of self is very prominent and visible in the nature of childhood experiences that girls have. Matrimonial relationships are seen in to induce most women an internalization of male superiority and the need for women's compliance and adjustment. *Gowri Ammal* believes in the supremacy of the husband's authority to exercise violence on his wife. She considered as a husband has all the rights to crush and tyrannize his wife and also beat her. But the wife has to serve him, it is her duty, worship and have to cherish him. Girija's conflicts stem from her domestic oppression. Girija is unable to partake in her children's joys fully because of her madi routine. When they brought snacks home, instead of enjoying them, she asked them to keep themselves away from her. Girija's husband Swaminathan, is oblivious of her needs and comforts. She is treated as a domestic servant whose duty is only to wash his pile of dirty clothes and iron them when he came back from his tour to make things ready even at a short notice before he left for the trip. While *Swaminathan*'s routine remained unperturbed, it was

Girija who had to make a lot of adjustments and sacrifices. In return for all that she did for him, he denied her the right to ask even a simple question. A week assertion on her partused to enrage him. He is unable to appreciate his wife's contribution to their ostensible domestic welfare.

According to the researcher in Lamps in the Whirlpool Girija has to struggle for the basic needs of herself as a wife to ask some questions about her life, children and also her husband about his role in the family. She has gone away without thinking of her children and their future, as a mother she has to analyze her role in the family and also struggle for self-identity in the family. Without thinking of the family, she left the home and became a brave woman. In her family life, she followed all the customs of her culture, tradition and custom without the mutual understanding between herself and her husband. Basic bond of love missing in her life, she might discuss with her feelings towards her husband and make him to understand. Then only life has to blossom in a perfect manner. Culture is one part of our life, apart from that love and the understanding playing a vital role in every man's life. In their life, there is no harmony and peace

Reference

G.R.Sharma:Indian Writing in English (Views and Reviews), Swastik Publications,
NewDelhi, 2013.

Dr.B.K.Jha:Modern Indian Writing in English, ALP Books,7/33,Ansari Road,Daryaganj, New Delhi,2011,Print

Ross Mandy:20thCentury Perspectives The Changing Role of Women, Reed Educational and Professional publishing Ltd, 2002, Print.

Watson, Lillian Eichler, (ed.), Lights from Many Lamps, New York, A Fireside

Book, Simon and Schuster, 1951.Print.

Williams, Haydn Moore, Indo-Anglian Literature, 1800-1970, A Survey,
Madras, Orient Longman, 1976.Print.

Williams, Haydn Moore, Studies in Modern Indian Fiction,Calcutta, A Writers
Workshop Greybird Book, 1973.Print.

Walsh, William, A Human Idiom: Literature and Humanity, London, Chatto and
Windus, 1964.Print.

CHAPTER FOUR

Feminist Perspective In Arundhati Roy'S The God Of Small Things

Arundhati Roy is a famous Indian novelist and social activist. She came into the limelight in 1997 when she won the Booker Prize for her first novel *The God of Small Things*. She was awarded Sydney Peace Prize in 2004. She was born November 24, 1961 in Assam. Her mother was a Keralite Christian and her father was a Bengali Hindu. Their marriage was not successful and *Arundhati Roy* spent her childhood years in *Aymanam,* Kerala with her mother. *Arundhati*'s mother, who was a prominent social activist, founded an independent school and taught her daughter informally. At age of sixteen *Arundhati Roy* left home, and eventually enrolled at the Delhi School of Architecture. There she met her first husband, *Gerard Da Cunha*, a fellow architecture student. Their marriage lasted four years. Both of them did not have a great love for architecture, so they quit their profession and went off to Goa. They used to make the cake and sell it on the beach to make living. This continued for seven months after which Arundhati returned back to Delhi.

She took a job at the *National Institute of Urban Affairs*, rented a *Darsati* near the dargah at *Nizamuddin* and hired a bicycle. One day film director *Pradeep Krishen* saw her cycling down a street and offered her a small role as a tribal girl in the film "*Massey Saab*". She accepted the role after initial reservations. She, later on, married Pradeep Krishen. Meanwhile, she got a scholarship to go to Italy for eight months to study the restoration of monuments. After returning from Italy *Arundhati Roy* linked with her husband to plan a 26 episode television serial for Doordarshan called the *Banyan Tree*. The serial was later scrapped. She wrote screenplays for a couple of TV films - *"In Which Annie Gives It Those Ones"* and *"Electric Moon"*. Arundhati Roy also wrote screenplay for *Shekhar Kapur's* controversial film *'Bandit Queen'*. The controversy escalated into a court case, after which Arundhati Roy retired to private life to concentrate on her writing, which eventually resulted in *The God of Small Things.*

After winning the Booker Prize for *"The God of Small Things"*, Arundhati Roy has concentrated her writings on political issues. She has written on varied topics such as the Narmada Dam project, India's nuclear weapons and American power giant Enron's activities in India. Arundhati Roy is strongly associated with the anti-globalization movement and is a staunch critic of neo-imperialism.

The God of Small Things was a fascinating story making the point that the small things in life are the more important things. The novel was very difficult to understand, but as the end of the novel approached the pieces of the puzzle began to fit together and make sense. The overall perspective of this novel relates to the simple and small things in life. So, what exactly does the title, *The God of Small Things*, signify to begin, the storyline takes place in *Ayemenem*, India. Roy purposely goes from the present to the past constantly to let history unfold in an unsystematic fashion. The plot is about a dysfunctional family who crosses each other's comfort zones and breaks the cultural norms of India in all different standpoints. The children, Estha and Rahel, are twins and are caught in the entanglements of adult corruption. They are constantly getting punished for being children, and are mimicking their mother, *Ammu*, in a different sort of way. The twins question if they should be sexually active with one another, while Ammu is being sexually active with an untouchable that is a friend of the family. Another possibility that could be running through the twin's heads is the fact that their mother is doing something that is not allowed by the Indian culture, so why can't they? These are the small things that make the picture of life itself.

Very soon *Ammu* started to feel hammed in by the restrictive atmosphere of the house worst of all were Pappachi's out bursts of physical violence inflicted on Mammachi from time to time. He beat his wife with a brass flower vase every night till Chacko slept in and stopped it forever. He, then smashed his favorite Mahoganj rocking chain with a plumber's monkey wrench because of a growing sense of frustration emanating from a blank retired life, more so, because of Mammachi's success as a violinist and her popularity in the pickle making business. Between the house and the river lies the family business *paradise pickle preserves.*

As a young girl, *Baby Kochamma* had fallen in love with Father Mulligan, a young Irish priest who had come to *Ayemenem* to study Hindu scriptures. In order to get closer to him, *Baby Kochamma*, against her father's wishes, became a Roman Catholic and joined a convent. It then became apparent that she couldn't compete with the others there, for his attention. Physically sick - because of convent food, lonely and depressed, she wrote several times to her parents. Her father eventually pulled her out, and sent her to the US for education, since, to his mind, no one would accept her as a wife anyway. She came back, two years later with a degree in ornamental gardening, extremely large, and still in love with Father *Mulligan*. (Father Mulligan later converts to Hinduism). Because of her own misfortunes, Baby Kochamma delights in the misfortune of others. She also hates those whom she sees as unfortunate.

While taking a pause at an aunt's place in Calcutta, she encountered a gentle Hindu Bengali from the tea estates in Assam and without further consideration consented to marry him. The charm of material bliss soon evaporated and *Ammu* became a victim of her husband's drunken rages. When they started to affect the two years old twins, Ammu thought it proper to desert her husband. At the age of 24 as a divorced daughter, she had no locusts Stand in her parental house. Yet she was weighed down by her millstones.

She likes to be perfect in children brought up. Rahel was frightened by the way Ammu said, "clean and dirty "so loudly. It is a great irony that a daughter estranged from her husband in this novel is tortured and tyrannized in the parent's house. While an estranged son, *Chacko* not only receives a warm welcome but also remains the rightful inheritor of the family's wealth and fortune. When he flirts with the labour class women of the factory, *Mammachi* and *Baby Kochamma*, encourage him in the name of "Man's Needs". But I see that the same behavior of *Ammu*, in her illicit relation with *Velutha*, is termed as untraditional and sinful. She is being locked in a room and is beaten black and blue. The codes of society make a great difference between men and women.

Both *Ammu* and *Chacko* find themselves in a similar position as far as their marital status is concerned. *Ammu* had been a victim of physical abuse while Chacko had been dumped by his wife for his slothful, barren ways. But in *Ayemenem, Chacko* rules the roast, being a male and *Ammu* lives at his mercy for her and her children's subsistence. *Margret Kochamma* was working as a waitress at a café in oxford where she first met Chacko and fell in love. Her father refused to attend the wedding because he disliked Indians. Both of them moved to condone a year into the marriage and the charm of Chacko's sudden sloth was off for *Margret Kochamma*. She had just discovered that she was pregnant when she met *Joe*. He was an old school friend of her brother. When they meet, Margret Kochamma was physically at her most attractive. *Joe* was a biologist. He was updating the third edition of a dictionary of biology for a small publishing house. *Joe* was everything that *Chacko* wasn't. When *Chacko* finished his badly paid assignment with the overseas sales department of the Indian Tea Board and couldn't find another job, he wrote of *Mamaachi,* telling her of his marriage and asking for money. By the time *Sophie Mol* was born, *Margret Kochamma* realized that for herself and her daughter's sake, she had to leave Chacko. She asked him for a divorce, *Chacko* returned to India where he found a job easily. She wrote regularly giving *Chacko* news of *Sophie Mol.* She assured him that *Joe* made a wonderful, caring father and that *Sophie Mol* loved him dearly. She was happy with Joe. When *Sophie Mol* was old enough to go to school, she enrolled herself in a teacher training course and then got a job as a junior school teacher in *Clapham*. She heard about *Joe*'s accident through a young policeman. At the time Chacko wrote inviting her to *Ayemenem*.

Sophie Mol and her mother *Margret* finally arrive. The family is at the airport to receive them. *Mamaachi* is waiting to receive them all. Though blind, she still manages to play the violin for Sophie. *Kochu Maria*, the maid, has baked a cake for Sophie. Little Sophie Mol wakes in Chacko's room and feels lovely and homesick. The three children *Estha, Rahel and Sophie Mol* are on the river bank. They put their little boat into the water. They are running away from home. They put extra provisions in the little boat for two weeks. The twins remember *Ammu*'s angry words when she sends them away. Sophie Mol has convinced *Estha and Rahel* to let her come along with them. The three of into the boat and start crossing the river.

The opening pages of the novel narrate *Rahel*'s return to *Ayemenem* after twenty-three years and then flashback to describe the funeral of Sophie Mol, without divulging the circumstances of her death.*Sophie Mol* is thereby established as a subaltern character. The circumstances leading to her drowning, the reader later finds out, were very different than what was said in the aftermath of her drowning: she had approached the river because she had, out of loneliness and a desire to escape the world of adults, convinced *Rahel* and *Estha* to let her come along, but *Margaret Kochamma* later interpreted *Estha* and *Rahel* as being responsible for her daughter's death. At the moment of her death, *Sophie Mol* became subject to radical re-interpretation that did not account for her own wishes and desires in life. Her identity was re-defined by her death instead of her life: "*Sophie Mol* became a Memory, while the Loss of *Sophie Mol* grew robust and alive" (253). It is the fact of *Sophie Mol's* loneliness and spirit of subtle protest against an adult world that the funeral effectively buried, and this was possibly one reason for *Sophie Mol's* posthumous screams during the funeral.

The drowning of *Sophie Mol* in the *Meenachal,* the reader finds out much later, did not allow even the slightest scream:

There was no storm-music. No whirlpool spun up from the inky depths of the Meenachal. No shark supervised the tragedy. Just a quiet handing-over ceremony. A boat spilling its cargo. A river accepting the offering. One small life. A brief sunbeam. With a silver thimble clenched for luck in its little fist (277).

The incident is a coming-together of the twin associations of the Meenachal River with boundary transgression and with silence. It is in or around the Meenachal River that deviant acts against the social order are performed, but these deviant acts in the end lead to punishment by the more powerful upholders of that social order. However, punishment is a silent, negative act of purging, forgetting, and washing away. Even though the death of Sophie Mol is purely accidental, the incident strongly interacts in the text with the figurative washing-away of Velutha.

Indeed, the brutal beating by the police of a helpless *Velutha,* the novel's only instance of bloody violence, is dealt with silently and efficiently. When Sophie's body is discovered, Baby *Kochamma* goes to the police and accuses *Velutha* of being responsible for Sophie's death. She claims that *Velutha* attempted to rape *Ammu,* threatened the family, and kidnapped the children. A group of policemen hunt *Velutha* down and savagely beat him for crossing caste lines. The twins witness this terrible scene and are deeply affected.

When the twins reveal the truth of Sophie's death to the chief of police, he is alarmed. He knows that *Velutha* is a communist, and is afraid that the wrongful arrest and impending death of *Velutha* will cause a riot amongst the local communists. He threatens Baby *Kochamma*, telling her that unless she gets the children to change their story, she will be held responsible for falsely accusing *Velutha* of the crime. Baby *Kochamma* tricks *Rahel* and *Estha* into believing that unless they accuse *Velutha* of Sophie's death, they and *Ammu* will all be sent to jail. *Estha* bears an even heavier burden when at the police station he is called in to respond "yes" to police questioning that will reveal *Velutha* as guilty. Not only does he carry the extra guilt of being forced into testifying against *Velutha*, but he also sees the aftermath of the police beating. *Velutha* dies from his injure.

After the funeral, *Ammu* took the twins back to the *Kottayam* police station. They were familiar with the place. They had spent a good part of the previous day there. Anticipating the sharp, smoky stink of old urine that permeated the walls and furniture, they clamped their nostrils shut well before the smell began. *Ammu* asked for the Station House Officer, and when she was shown into his office, she told him that there had been a terrible mistake and that she wanted to make a statement. She asked to see Velutha. Inspector *Thomas Mathew's* mustaches bustled like the friendly Air India Maharajah's, but his eyes were sly and greedy. It's a little too late for all this, don't you think?" he said. He spoke the coarse *Kottayam* dialect of Malayalam. He stared at *Ammu's* breasts as he spoke. He said the police knew all they needed to know and that the Kottayam Police didn't take statements from vesbyas or their illegitimate children. *Ammu* said she'd see about that. Inspector Thomas Mathew came around his desk and approached *Ammu* with his baton.

'If I were you," he said, "I'd go home quietly.' Then he tapped her breasts with his baton. As though he was choosing mangoes from a basket. Pointing out the ones that he wanted to be packed and delivered. Inspector Thomas Mathew seemed to know whom he could pick on and whom he couldn't.

When they left the police station Ammu was crying, it was the first time they'd seen their mother cry. She wasn't sobbing. Her face was set like stone, but the tears welled up in her eyes and ran down her rigid cheeks. It made the twins sick with feat Ammu's tears made everything that had so far seemed unreal, rcal. They went back to *Ayemenem* by bus. However, Baby *Kochamma* has underestimated *Ammu*'s love for *Velutha*. Hearing of his arrest, *Ammu* goes to the police, to tell the truth about their relationship. The policemen abuse her and ask her to leave the matter alone. Afraid of being exposed, Baby *Kochamma* convinces Chacko to believe that *Ammu* and the twins are responsible for his daughter's death. Chacko forces *Ammu* to leave the house. *Ammu*, unable to find a job, is forced to send *Estha* to live with his father. *Estha* never sees *Ammu* again, as she dies alone and impoverished a few years later. *Rahel,* when grown up, leaves for the US, get married, divorced and finally returns to *Ayemenem* after several years of working as a waitress in an Indian restaurant and as a night clerk at a gas station. *Rahel* and *Estha,* both 31 at this time, are reunited for the first time since they were 7 years old. Both *Estha* and *Rahel* have been damaged by their past, and by this time *Estha* has become perpetually silent because of his traumatic childhood.

Arundhati Roy has shown her sympathetic and revolutionary attitude, especially to the neglected women and untouchable workers in this novel. The prominent theme she raises in this book is the realistic delineation of the plight of women in society. The other prominent theme of the novel, which merits our attention much, is the author's truthful portrayal of untouchability, a fatal infectious disease, which prevents the development of society. Right from the Vedic age up to this time, the untouchables in society have been bearing the brunt of social persecution without any rhyme or reason. The women and the untouchable and which are still operative in a large part of India, Roy brings a fresh perspective to bear on an age –old subject. However, it is also worth considering how women act as agents of this society and help in the undoing of another woman. Even women, who had been deprived in their own life, and could not disturb society in the least, preferred to come down on another woman with all the unspent rage of their frustration like Ammu's mother Sosha Komachi. In 'The *God Of Small'* the novelist implicitly advocates greater social reform in the riged positioning of women. The world of Arundhati Roy's novel is captured in a state of flux where the values of the patriarchal society are under attack from a new world in which self-interest and self-garnishment and social equality are forcing their entry seen from a feminist point of view the novel speaks of the violence perpetrated upon women and paternal tyranny engulfing the luckless children. It ruthlessly unmasks the dual standards of morality in society in respect of men and women, the passive, submissive role of a wife in a man – women relationship, and the vindictive attitude of a woman in prolonging the suffering and ignominy of another woman by a male. *The God of Small Things* is not a novel about mass struggle. Rather, it is about the ways which individuals, particularly women, find to resist the conditions imposed upon them by society.

REFERENCES

- Kolhatkar, Sonali and Arundhati Roy. “Superstars and Globalization: Interviewing Arundhati Roy.” Published online at Z Communications:
- Rana, Swati. “Arundhati Roy: On Writing and Politics.” Main Street. Vol 2. No. 1 Fall 2004.
- Roy, Arundhati. “Do Turkeys Enjoy Thanksgiving?” and “Instant-Mix Imperial Democracy.” An Ordinary Person’s Guide to Empire. Cambridge, MA: South End Press, 2004.
- Sathyamala, C. “The Emperor’s New Clothes: The God of Small Things.” Arundhati Roy: The Novelist Extraordinary. Dhawan, R.K. Ed. London: Sangam Books, 1999.
- Roy, Arundhati. “Come September.” War Talk. Cambridge, MA: South End Press, 2003.Roy, Arundhati. Come September. AK Press Audio, 2004.
- Sontheimer, Michael. “‘Everything is being violated: An interview with the Indian writer Arundhati Roy on the war in Iraq and global resistance against American hegemony.
- Dodiya, Jaydipsinh, and Joya Chakravarty, *The Critical Studies of Arundhati Roy’s “The God of Small Things,”* Atlantic Publishers & Distributors, 1999.

9 798887 172224

Printed by Libri Plureos GmbH in Hamburg,
Germany